CD INCLUDED

TROMBONE

HAL•LEONARD
BIG BAND
PLAY-ALONG
VOLUME 4

Jazz Classics

T0056188

ISBN 978-1-4234-4987-4

HAL•LEONARD®
CORPORATION
7777 W. BLUEMOUND RD. P.O. BOX 13819 MILWAUKEE, WI 53213

Visit Hal Leonard Online at
www.halleonard.com

CD INCLUDED

HAL·LEONARD

BIG BAND PLAY-ALONG

VOLUME 4

Jazz Classics

BAGS' GROOVE

By MILT JACKSON
Arranged by MARK TAYLOR

TROMBONE

TROMBONE

BLUE 'N BOOGIE

Trombone

By JOHN "DIZZY" GILLESPIE and FRANK PAPARELLI
Arranged by MARK TAYLOR

TROMBONE

BLUE TRAIN
(BLUE TRANE)

By JOHN COLTRANE
Arranged by MARK TAYLOR

TROMBONE

8

TROMBONE

DOXY

TROMBONE

By SONNY ROLLINS
Arranged by MARK TAYLOR

TROMBONE

FOUR

By MILES DAVIS
Arranged by MARK TAYLOR

TROMBONE

TROMBONE

MOTEN SWING

By BUSTER MOTEN and BENNIE MOTEN
Arranged by SAMMY NESTICO

TROMBONE

TROMBONE

OLEO

By SONNY ROLLINS
Arranged by MARK TAYLOR

TROMBONE

TROMBONE

SONG FOR MY FATHER

TROMBONE

Words and Music by HORACE SILVER
Arranged by MARK TAYLOR

TROMBONE

STOLEN MOMENTS

Words and Music by OLIVER NELSON
Arranged by MARK TAYLOR

TROMBONE

TROMBONE

STRAIGHT NO CHASER

By THELONIOUS MONK
Arranged by MARK TAYLOR

TROMBONE

TROMBONE

THE BIG BAND PLAY-ALONG SERIES

These revolutionary play-along packs are great products for those who want a big band sound to back up their instrument, without the pressure of playing solo. They're perfect for current players and for those former players who want to get back in the swing!

Each volume includes:

- Easy-to-read, authentic big band arrangements
- Professional recordings on CD of all the big band instruments, including the lead part
- Editions for alto sax, tenor sax, trumpet, trombone, guitar, piano, bass, and drums

1. SWING FAVORITES

April in Paris • I've Got You Under My Skin • In the Mood • It Don't Mean a Thing (If It Ain't Got That Swing) • Route 66 • Speak Low • Stompin' at the Savoy • Tangerine • This Can't Be Love • Until I Met You (Corner Pocket).

07011313	Alto Sax	$14.95
07011314	Tenor Sax	$14.95
07011315	Trumpet	$14.95
07011316	Trombone	$14.95
07011317	Guitar	$14.95
07011318	Piano	$14.95
07011319	Bass	$14.95
07011320	Drums	$14.95

2. POPULAR HITS

Ain't No Mountain High Enough • Brick House • Copacabana (At the Copa) • Evil Ways • I Heard It Through the Grapevine • On Broadway • Respect • Street Life • Yesterday • Zoot Suit Riot.

07011321	Alto Sax	$14.95
07011322	Tenor Sax	$14.95
07011323	Trumpet	$14.95
07011324	Trombone	$14.95
07011325	Guitar	$14.95
07011326	Piano	$14.95
07011327	Bass	$14.95
07011328	Drums	$14.95

3. DUKE ELLINGTON

Caravan • Chelsea Bridge • Cotton Tail • I'm Beginning to See the Light • I'm Just a Lucky So and So • In a Mellow Tone • In a Sentimental Mood • Mood Indigo • Satin Doll • Take the "A" Train.

00843086	Alto Sax	$14.95
00843087	Tenor Sax	$14.95
00843088	Trumpet	$14.95
00843089	Trombone	$14.95
00843090	Guitar	$14.95
00843091	Piano	$14.95
00843092	Bass	$14.95
00843093	Drums	$14.95

4. JAZZ CLASSICS

Bags' Groove • Blue 'N Boogie • Blue Train (Blue Trane) • Doxy • Four • Moten Swing • Oleo • Song for My Father • Stolen Moments • Straight No Chaser.

00843094	Alto Sax	$14.95
00843095	Tenor Sax	$14.95
00843096	Trumpet	$14.95
00843097	Trombone	$14.95
00843098	Guitar	$14.95
00843099	Piano	$14.95
00843100	Bass	$14.95
00843101	Drums	$14.95

HAL•LEONARD® CORPORATION

7777 W. BLUEMOUND RD. P.O. BOX 13819 MILWAUKEE, WI 53213

Prices, contents and availability subject to change without notice.